Helping Children See Jesus

ISBN: 978-1-64104-035-8

Wisdom
Old Testament Volume 31:
Proverbs, Ecclesiastes, Song of Solomon

Author: Arlene S Piepgrass
Illustrator: Vernon Henkel
Colorization: Olivia and Bethany Moy
Typesetting and Layout: Patricia Pope

© 2019 Bible Visuals International
PO Box 153, Akron, PA 17501-0153
Phone: (717) 859-1131
www.biblevisuals.org

All rights reserved. No part of this publication may be reproduced, stored in a retrieval system or transmitted in any form by any means, electronic, mechanical, photocopy, recording or otherwise, without the prior permission of the publisher, except as provided by USA copyright law.

RELATED ITEMS

To access related items (such as activities, memory verse posters and translated texts) please visit our web store at www.biblevisuals.org and enter 2031 in the search box at the top right of the web page. You may need to reduce the zoom setting to get the search box.

FREE TEXT DOWNLOAD

To obtain a FREE printable copy of the teaching text (PDF format) please scroll down and select Extra–PDF Teacher Text Download to place in your shopping cart. When checking out, use coupon code XTACSV17 at checkout. Under Product Format select English and click on Apply Coupon for the discount. Other languages are available at an additional cost.

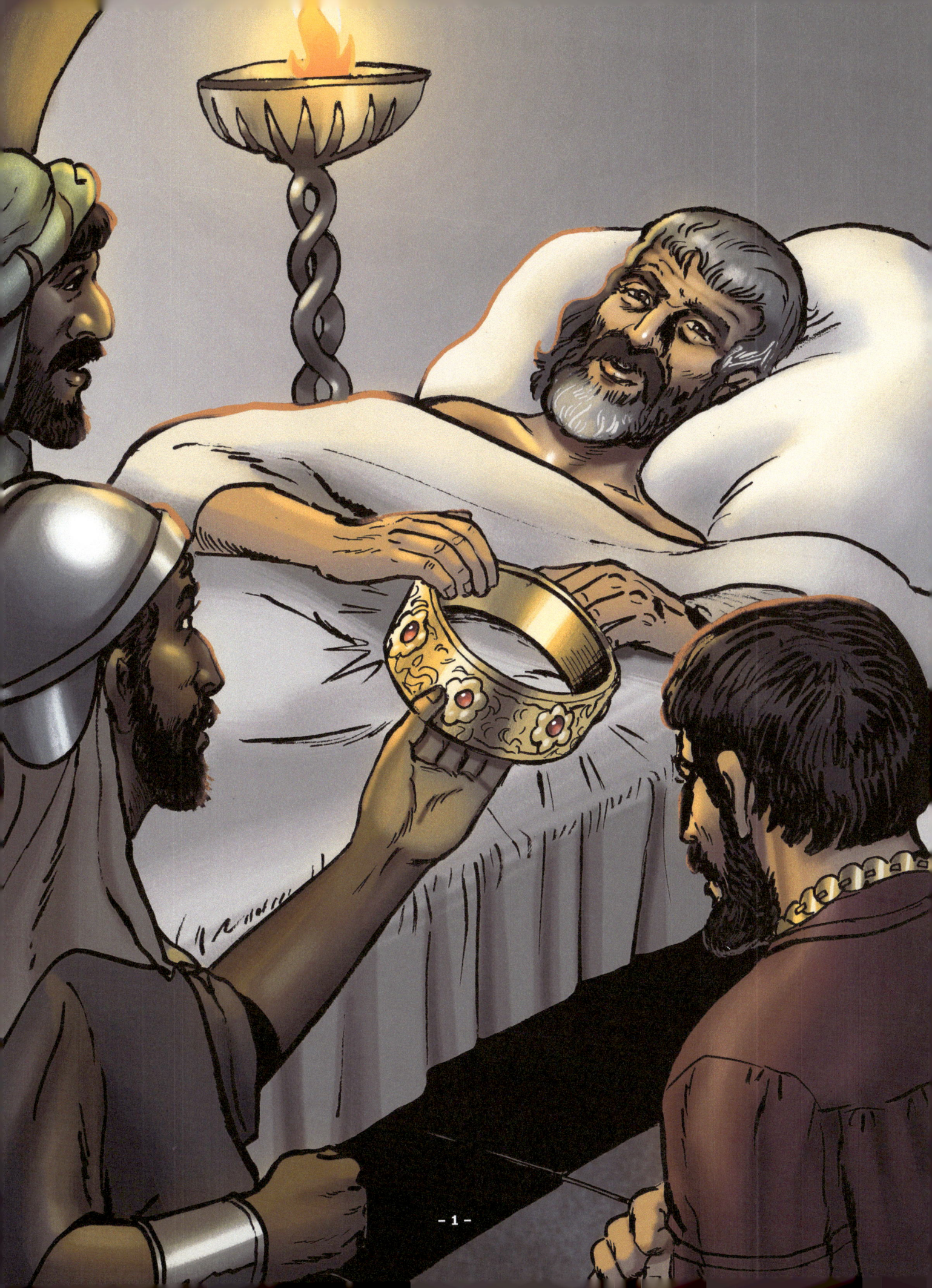

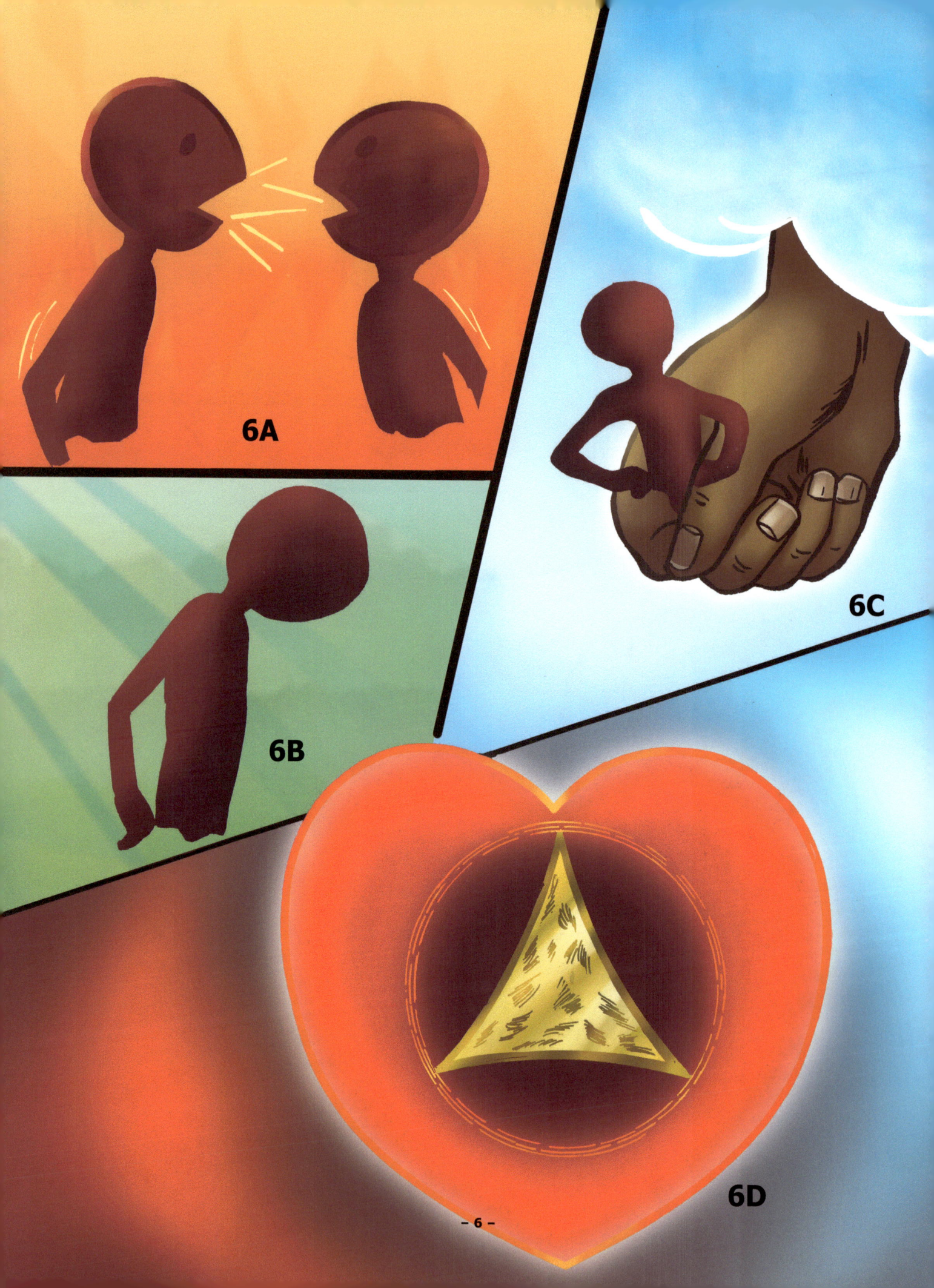

The fear of the LORD is the beginning of wisdom and knowledge of the Holy is understanding.

Proverbs 9:10

Lesson 1
WISDOM FROM GOD

NOTE TO THE TEACHER

God's Holy Spirit caused Solomon to write the books of Proverbs, Ecclesiastes and The Song of Solomon. (See 2 Peter 1:21.) "Solomon's wisdom was greater than the wisdom of all the men of the East and greater than all the wisdom of Egypt. He was wiser than any other man . . . And his fame spread to all the surrounding nations. He spoke 3,000 proverbs and his songs numbered 1005" (1 Kings 4:32). We have much to learn from Solomon's wise teachings.

The subject of our study, *WISDOM*, is "the fear of the LORD" (Proverbs 9:10). To fear Him is to trust, reverence and obey Him. In Proverbs, God says those who fear the LORD are wise. Those who do not fear Him live as if there is no God. Lacking good sense, they are called "fools." (See Proverbs 28:26; Psalm 14:1.)

God's wisdom enables His people to live lives which honor Him. (See Proverbs 2:6; 8:17; James 1:5.) Keep before your students that we all make choices. These choices determine: (1) Whether or not God will be honored and pleased by our conduct and (2) Where we shall spend eternity.

The book of Proverbs teaches us how to live wisely. God's wisdom guides us in our relationships with others. His widom directs us to have pure thoughts. When we have God's wisdom we do not offend His holiness. Nor do we dishonor other Christians.

In this study of Solomon's three books, we also focus on his life. Have you taught Old Testament Volume 23, *A Kingdom Forever*? If so, review highlights of the first two lessons to introduce this volume. If your students know local proverbs, have them quote some. Then they will quickly understand the use of biblical proverbs.

On illustration #3a, print WISE on dotted line at top left. On illustration 3b top right dotted line, print FOOLISH. Keep page covered, revealing each illustration as you mention it.

At top center of illustration #4, print MAKING CHOICES. On 4a, in bright cloud, print RIGHT. On 4b, in dark cloud, print WRONG.

Scripture to be studied: 1 Kings 1-4; 2 Chronicles 1; Proverbs (see lesson)

The *aim* of the lesson: To show that wisdom from God is our greatest treasure.

What your students should *know*: To be wise is to fear the Lord.

What your students should *feel*: The need for God's wisdom in making choices.

What your students should *do*: Ask God for wisdom to make right choices this week.

Lesson outline (for the teacher's and students' notebooks):
1. Solomon, the king (1 Kings 1:1-2:12).
2. Solomon's choice (1 Kings 3:4-15; 4:29-34; 2 Chronicles 1:7-12).
3. Solomon's teaching (See verses in lesson).
4. Solomon's advice (See verses in lesson).

The verse to be memorized:

The fear of the LORD is the beginning of wisdom and knowledge of the Holy is understanding.
 (Proverbs 9:10)

THE LESSON:

Suppose someone said to you, "I shall give you anything you want." What would you choose? (Encourage response.)

In the long ago (almost 3,000 years ago), God Himself said that to a young man. Let me tell you what happened.

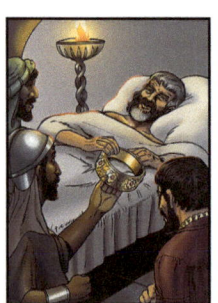

1. SOLOMON, THE KING
1 Kings 1:1-2:12

The young man was the son of Israel's great King David. King David loved God and almost always pleased Him. Finally David was old and sick. And he knew he was about to die.

Show Illustration #1

King David sent for three of his men. (See 1 Kings 1:1, 32-35.) Quietly he announced, "Make my son Solomon the new king. He will take my place, sit on my throne and wear the crown. Sound the trumpets (horns). Shout, 'God save King Solomon!'"

King David's servants immediately obeyed his orders. God's people (Israel and Judah) were delighted to have Solomon as their king. They wanted him to be safe and live a long time. So they celebrated, shouting, "God save King Solomon!"

Later, David called for King Solomon and talked to him. "My son," he began, "be strong. Obey all God's commands. Always do right. Take a stand against wrong."

Thoughtfully, David continued, "Many years ago God gave me a wonderful promise. He said that members of our family would always sit on Israel's throne. This can only be so, God said, *if* we do what is right. We must obey God's laws and be faithful to Him. (See 1 Kings 2:1-4.) Solomon, my son, learn to know the true and living God. Study His laws. Obey Him. Then our family can rule over this land forever. Remember, Solomon, the LORD (JEHOVAH, the Holy One who hates sin) sees your heart. He knows all your thoughts." (See 1 Chronicles 28:8-9.)

King David had given Solomon good advice: "Know God. Study His laws. Obey His commands." And this is good advice for us today.

2. SOLOMON'S CHOICE
1 Kings 3:4-15; 4:29-34; 2 Chronicles 1:7-12

King Solomon loved the LORD as his father had. He showed his love by offering sacrifices to God. God had commanded His people (the Israelites) to do this.

One day King Solomon led his people to God's altar (at Gibeon). There they worshiped the LORD. Solomon offered to God a tremendous gift of 1,000 animals! These were *burnt offerings*. (Teacher: Explain that burnt offerings showed he was setting himself apart, *consecrating* himself, to God.) Solomon loved God very much and was promising to do whatever God wanted.

- 18 -

That night the LORD appeared to Solomon in a dream. The LORD said, "Solomon, ask for whatever you want Me to give you."

Did you hear that? God Himself would give Solomon anything he asked for! What do you suppose Solomon wanted? (Let students make suggestions. Or ask: Money? Honor? A big house? The death of his enemies?)

Listen to what King Solomon prayed for. "Give me an understanding heart to know how to rule over Your people. Help me to know right from wrong." (See 1 Kings 3:6-9.) Solomon wanted to be a good, wise king. He longed to honor and obey the LORD.

God was pleased with the king's prayer. He said, "Solomon, you have asked for wisdom to rule over My people. So I shall make you very wise, the wisest person ever. I shall also give you what you did not ask for: riches and honor. No one in the world will be as rich and famous as you, Solomon." (See 1 Kings 3:1012; 2 Chronicles 1:11-12.)

God added another promise, a promise with an "if" in it. God said, "Solomon, do what I want you to do. Obey My laws as your father David did. *If* you do, I shall give you a long life." (See 1 Kings 3:14.) What was the "if" in God's promise? What would King Solomon have to do to live a long time? *(He would have to obey God's laws.)*

Did God have the right to say how Solomon should live? (Let students discuss.) Of course He did! God created everything and everyone, including you and me. (See Proverbs 3:19-20.) He who created us has the right to tell us how to live. And in His Word He explains the way to live.

Show Illustration #2
The LORD kept His promise to King Solomon and made him very wise. Because of Solomon's wisdom, many came to listen and learn from him. What they learned from Solomon was really from God. For it was God who gave Solomon wisdom to teach.

Do you wish you could have learned from wise King Solomon? I have good news for you. You *can* learn from him. Solomon wrote many of his wise teachings as proverbs. (A proverb is a short saying which teaches a fact.) God has kept Solomon's truths in the Bible book called Proverbs. Because they are in God's Word, they are God's message to *you*. (See 2 Timothy 3:16.) Indeed, Solomon begins many proverbs saying, "My son." *(Teacher: See, for example, Proverbs 1:8, 10, 15; 2:1; 3:1, 11, 21.)*

So wise King Solomon is teaching *you* as his own son or daughter.

3. SOLOMON'S TEACHING

Show Illustration 3A-1/B-1
King Solomon taught, "There are two kinds of people. Some are wise; others are foolish." All of us are in one of these groups. Either we are WISE (point to illustration 3A-1) or we are FOOLISH (point to illustration 3B-1).

Wise King Solomon explained, "The fear of the LORD is the beginning of wisdom" (Proverbs 1:7; 9:10). *(Teacher: Unless otherwise stated, all verses which follow are from Proverbs. Decide ahead of time which verses you should use. Print each verse and reference on a slip of paper. Have students read them to class at appropriate times.)*

Solomon spoke of "the fear of the LORD." Do *you* think he meant we are to be afraid of the LORD? Oh, no! The LORD loves us. He loves us so much He sent to earth His Son, Jesus Christ. Jesus Christ loved us so much He died for our sins. (Uncover illustration 3a-1. Quote John 3:16.) No, we are not afraid of such a loving LORD.

To fear the LORD is to worship Him, honor Him, trust Him. When we truly fear the LORD, we obey Him and hate evil (3:5-7; 8:13). Solomon said fearing the LORD is wisdom- it is being *wise*. You learn to fear the LORD by studying what He says in the Bible.

Show Illustration 3B-2
Do you fear the LORD? Do you love Him? Do you try to learn all you can about Him? Do you study and obey His Word? (See 1:5; 2:1-5; 4:5-13.) Are you wise?

Fools are those who refuse to study God's Word (1:7b). A foolish person ignores God's Word and His teaching (1:22).

Show Illustration 3B-2
A fool says, "There is no God" and lives as if there is no God. (See Psalm 14:1; 53:1; Proverbs 1:29-30.) A foolish person does wrong and hurts others (2:14). Foolish people refuse to believe Christ died for sinners.

Now *you* know the difference between wise and foolish people. Which are you? (Point to the words WISE/FOOLISH at top of illustration 3.) The choice is yours. But remember! The Lord knows your choice. He knows everything you do (15:3). He sees inside your heart. God knows if you have received the Lord Jesus into your heart and life.

Show Illustration 3B-3
Choosing the Lord Jesus as your Saviour is the wisest choice *you* can make. This is the only way *you* can be right with God. (Point to rays around heart and the word WISE. Read 4:18.) " . . . The path of the righteous [person] is like the shining light, which shines brighter and brighter . . ." The LORD blesses (gives good to) those who are wise (3:33b).

But listen to this from God: "The LORD'S curse is on fools" (3:33a). To close your heart to the Lord Jesus, is your most foolish, wicked choice. "The way of the wicked is like darkness" (4:19).

Show Illustration 3B-3
(Point to dark cloud around the word FOOLISH.) Do *you* want God's cursing or His blessing? The choice is yours.

4. SOLOMON'S ADVICE
There are other choices we make every day. For example, we choose our friends. Choosing friends is very important because we become like our friends.

Point to Illustration 4B-1
We do what our friends do, and go where they go. The person who has a wise friend [who fears the LORD] grows wise. The person who goes with fools will be in trouble (13:20.).

Wise Solomon said, "Stay far away from people who steal. They may say to *you*, 'Come help us, and what we steal, we shall share with *you*. You will get rich with all we steal from others.'"

Point to Illustration 4B-2

"Do not go with those who steal," King Solomon warned. "They will hurt or may kill innocent people. One day they will get caught. Then they themselves may be killed" (1:10-19).

"Do not make friends with a short-tempered person," God commanded through Solomon. "Do not go around with anyone who gets angry easily."

Point to Illustration 4B-3

"If *you* do, *you,* too can become short-tempered and angry." (See 22:24; 29:22.)

Solomon, the wise king, said sternly, "NEVER be a friend of those who get drunk" (20:1; 23:20a).

Point to Illustration 4B-4

"You will be tempted to do what they do. Then *you* will harm yourself and others."

So God has taught us, through Solomon, that we are to choose wise friends.

Point to Illustration 4A-2

We must also choose wise words. Each of us has a mouth. What do you do with your mouth and lips? (Encourage response.) Do you speak kind words?

Solomon says, "The LORD hates a lying tongue" (6:16-17). Are *you* ever tempted to lie? Remember, the LORD hates lies!

Point to Illustration 4B-4

We hurt others when we whisper harmfully (gossip) about them (16:28). Do *you* like it when others gossip about *you?* Of course not! So keep your mouth tightly shut whenever you are tempted to gossip or speak harmfully.

Point to Illustration 4A-2

Through Solomon God commands: "Think before you speak. Do not talk a lot (13:3). When you speak, say something which helps others" (10:19-21).

How do you answer someone who is angry with you? Do you answer angrily? Solomon says, "A soft, kind answer will turn away anger" (15:1, 2, 4). Try it the next time someone speaks angrily to *you.* It may not be easy. But the LORD can help you if you ask Him (15:29).

CONCLUSION

Do you remember King David's advice to his son Solomon? (Review from lesson point #1.) Know God. Study His laws. Obey His commands.

Point to Illustration 4A-3

Do you want God's blessing, His favor? Be wise. Study God's Word and obey it (19:20). Remember: "The path of the righteous [wise person], is like a shining light" (4:18).

Point to Illustration 4A-4

It leads to God's beautiful, shining home in Heaven.

Point to Illustration 4B-5

King Solomon solemnly warned, "The way of the wicked is like darkness" (4:19).

Wickedness and foolishness lead to death–separation from God forever (1:29-32). Are you a foolish person? Or will you be wise and choose God's way?

Teacher: Stress the importance of making wise choices in daily living. Emphasize the urgency of choosing to receive Jesus Christ as Saviour. Encourage students who wish to do so, to remain after class. Then talk with them personally.

Lesson 2
WISDOM FOR LIVING

NOTE TO THE TEACHER

God does not always give riches to those who fear *(reverence and obey)* Him. But He did bless Solomon this way. He also blessed him by allowing the nation of Israel to have peace and prosperity. (See 1 Kings 4:24-25; 5:4.) He blessed Solomon with world-wide fame. (See 1 Kings 4:34.) And God let Solomon see His glory cloud come from Heaven. (See 1 Kings 8:11; 2 Chronicles 5:14.)

Because Solomon and Israel obeyed God, He helped them. And He provided for them. (See 1 Kings 3:12; 5:12.) Solomon understood the danger of loving the blessings instead of God who gave them. So in Proverbs he warns against pride and the love of money. Solomon also emphasizes the importance of having one's heart right with God.

The verse to be memorized is not difficult. However, take time to explain it clearly. Continually remind your students of the necessity of fearing *(reverencing and obeying)* the LORD. This is the "beginning of wisdom." Without a proper attitude towards the Lord, we cannot be wise. And students and teacher must have "knowledge of the Holy One." Not to know who God is and what He does, is to be ignorant. Only by studying the Bible can we learn the wonders of God.

Do you have Old Testament Volume 23, *A Kingdom Forever?* If so, use illustrations 6, 7a and 7b with point #1 of this lesson.

Begin this lesson by reviewing the previous lesson-especially the characteristics of the wise and foolish. Use illustrations on pages 3 and 4. Answer questions which may have arisen about these subjects.

All Scripture references are in Proverbs, unless otherwise noted.

On illustration #6, print in large letters PRIDE on top dotted line. On illustration #8 (top dotted line) print MONEY.

Cut out two large hearts and paste edges together. Leave top open. Print one Bible verse and reference from each lesson truth. Place them inside heart. At conclusion of lesson, have each student draw out a verse and read it aloud. Have others in class tell which lesson truth the verse emphasizes.

Scripture to be studied: 1 Kings 5-10; 1 Chronicles 22, 28, 29; 2 Chronicles 2-9

The *aim* of the lesson: To show that God blesses those who live according to His wisdom.

What your students should *know*: The Lord is pleased with those who fear (reverence and obey) Him.

What your students should *feel*: A desire to please God in their daily living.

What your students should *do*: Choose to obey God this week in their thoughts and desires.

Lesson outline (for the teacher's and students' notebooks):
1. Solomon builds God's temple (1 Kings 5-9; 1 Chronicles 22, 28, 29).
2. Solomon warns against pride (See verses in lesson).
3. Solomon becomes famous (1 Kings 10; 2 Chronicles 9).
4. Solomon teaches about money (See verses in lesson).

The verse to be memorized:

The fear of the LORD is the beginning of wisdom and knowledge of the Holy is understanding. (Proverbs 9:10)

THE LESSON:

If God asked you to do something for Him, would you do it? Would you do something your father asked you to do? Sometimes God uses our Christian parents to give us His message. King Solomon knew it was wise to listen to godly parents. And he teaches us to listen to our parents, particularly those who love the Lord. (See Proverbs 1:8; 6:20; compare Exodus 20:12; Ephesians 6:2-3.)

1. SOLOMON BUILDS GOD'S TEMPLE
1 Kings 5-9; 1 Chronicles 22, 28, 29

Solomon honored and listened to his father, King David.

Show Illustration #5

Before his death, David had spoken seriously to Solomon, saying, "My son, I wanted to build a magnificent temple [of worship] for God. But God said, 'No, David. You cannot build a temple for Me. You have fought many wars. When your son Solomon is king, there will be peace in Israel. Then I shall have him build My temple.'" (See 1 Chronicles 22:5-10.)

King David continued, "Now, Solomon, you are to build God's temple. He will be with you. Be sure to obey the Lord, Solomon." (See 1 Chronicles 22:12-13; 28:20.)

King David died before the temple was begun. Yet King Solomon obeyed his father. He would have remembered his father's prayer: "Give to my son Solomon a perfect heart" (1 Chronicles 29:19).

With determination, Solomon made an announcement. "I shall build a great temple for the LORD my God. Our God is great, the greatest of all. Who can build a place worthy of Him? Even the highest heavens cannot hold Him. But we shall be able to worship Him at His temple." (See 2 Chronicles 2:4a, 5-6.)

It was an honor for King Solomon to be responsible for building the temple. But he was neither proud nor puffed-up about it. He was simply thankful to be chosen to do something for God.

The people of God gave everything needed for the temple. Thousands worked hard to build it. Finally, seven years later, the temple was completed. It was magnificent! The walls and wooden floors were covered with gold. All the furniture was gold-covered.

The priests brought God's precious old ark to the temple courtyard. There King Solomon stood with crowds of people. More sheep and oxen were sacrificed than could be counted. Together the people worshiped the Lord God of Heaven.

Then the priests solemnly carried the ark into the most holy place. Carefully, they set it down and left.

Outside, in the courtyard, the priests joined the musicians. Trumpeters (120 of them!) played their horns along with those who played other instruments. And the singers sang: "God is good; His love lasts forever." (See 2 Chronicles 5:12-13.) Oh, how they sang!

The Lord, watching from Heaven, was pleased. So His cloud came down. This was God's glorious, holy presence, and it filled the temple. (See 2 Chronicles 5:13-14.) All the people fell down and worshiped the Lord. It was a wonderful day!

2. SOLOMON WARNS AGAINST PRIDE

King Solomon could have felt puffed up with pride that day. He could have said, "Look at the beautiful temple I have built. See how great *I* am!" He knew how easy it is to be proud.

Do you know what pride is? (Encourage student response.) To be proud is to boast about yourself. Pride causes you to feel important or satisfied with yourself. Pride makes you want to be praised by others. When you cannot admit you are wrong, you are proud.

Through King Solomon's proverbs, we learn what God says about pride. "Pride causes arguments and quarrels." (See 13:10.)

Show Illustration 6A

People who speak foolishly are proud. (See 14:3.)

Says King Solomon: "When pride comes, then comes shame. Pride will bring a person low." (See 11:2; 29:23.)

Show Illustration 6B

Now hear this proverb: "Pride goes before destruction." (See 16:18; 18:12.) God "hates a proud look" and pride inside your heart. (See 6:16-17; 16:5.) If you are proud, God will punish you in His own way.

Show Illustration 6C

You may not act like a proud person. But if pride is in your heart, God sees it. For He sees and knows everything about you.

Pride causes some people to say, "I do not need God. I can get along without Him." This is the opposite of fearing *(reverencing and obeying]* the LORD. Do you think proud people are WISE or FOOLISH? *(Foolish.)*

God hates pride. But He is pleased with His own who are humble. That is, they are not puffed up with pride. They do not speak or act foolishly. They do not boast about themselves. Nor do they expect to be praised by others.

God says this about the humble: "They take advice and become wise" (13:10). Humble people speak wisely (14:3). The humble person will receive honor. (See 15:33; 18:12; 22:4; 29:23.) Humble people may not be honored here on earth. But how wonderful it will be when they are rewarded in Heaven!

Solomon was the richest man of his time. Yet he taught, "It is better to be poor and humble than to be rich and proud" (15:16; 16:19; 17:1). Solomon was not proud. At this time, his heart was right with God. That is, he loved God. His thoughts pleased God. What he did pleased God.

In Solomon's proverbs, he spoke of our hearts. (See 4:23; 23:12, 15, 17, 19, 24-26.) Solomon was not talking about our hearts which pump blood through our bodies. He was speaking of something deep inside us which affects everything we do. Perhaps you call it your "conscience."

God created each of us with a conscience–something which tells us right from wrong.

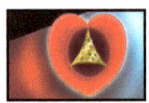

Show Illustration 6D

A man who did know God described his conscience this way: "It is a three cornered piece of metal in my heart. When I do wrong, the metal turns and makes a little groove which hurts. But finally, after having done many wrongs, the groove is deep. And the corner of the metal is worn down. So now, when I sin, it hardly hurts at all."

King Solomon commanded, "Guard your heart" (4:23). How can you guard your heart, your conscience? (Let students discuss.) King David (Solomon's father) said, "God's Word have I hidden in my heart so I might not sin against Him" (Psalm 119:11). Wise Solomon said we are to write God's commands on the tablet of our hearts. (See 3:1-3; 7:1-3.) How do we do this? *(We read, study and memorize God's Word.)* God's Word should be more precious to us than anything else.

When you know the teachings of God's Word, your heart will control your thoughts. It will keep you from saying bad words. God's Word in your heart will guard you. You will be kept from listening to sinful programs on radio or television. God's Word in your heart will protect you. You will not want to look at sinful pictures or read bad books.

God's Word in your heart will shield you from wrong-doing:

1. It will help you to say "no" when you are tempted to take drugs. (See 1 Corinthians 3:16; 6:19-20; Galatians 5:20 (the word "sorcery" is the use of drugs).)
2. God's Word will help you to say "no" to drinking anything intoxicating. (See 4:14-17; 20:1; 23:29-32; Romans 14:21.)
3. If someone asks you to commit immoral sex, you will be able to say "no" when you have God's Word in your heart. (See 2:10-22.)
4. God's Word will guide you if others try to get you into trouble. (See 1:8-16; 3:21-26.)

When you know and love God's Word, you will choose to do right. You will want to say, "Yes, Lord, I shall obey You."

3. SOLOMON BECOMES FAMOUS
1 Kings 10; 2 Chronicles 9

(Teacher:' Review Solomon's request for wisdom and God's promise, Lesson. #1.)

God always keeps His promises. He kept His promise to King Solomon. God made Solomon greater, richer and wiser than all other kings. Everyone wanted to hear the wisdom God had placed in his heart. (See 1 Kings 10:23-24.)

Even a queen visited King Solomon. She lived in Sheba, far, far from Jerusalem. (About 1,200 miles–almost 2,000 kilometers.) She kept hearing about the wise, rich King Solomon. Finally she decided to see if what she heard was true.

Show Illustration #7

The queen of Sheba was very rich herself. So she came with pack animals loaded with wonderful gifts for King Solomon. She saw Solomon's palace, his many servants, the magnificent temple he had built. And she was amazed!

Later she told King Solomon, "I did not believe you were so wise, not until I talked with you. Now I know you are even greater than I was told. Those around you are blessed [favored] to hear your wisdom." (See 1 Kings 10:1-9; 2 Chronicles 9:1-8.)

Like the queen of Sheba, we, too, are blessed by wise King Solomon. How glad we are for his wonderful book of Proverbs!

4. SOLOMON TEACHES ABOUT MONEY

King Solomon was the richest man of his day. So, in his proverbs, he says much about money. Why is money important-what is it used for? (Encourage student discussion.) Is money something good? *(Yes, we need it to live.)* How do people usually get money? *(By working)*

Show Illustration 8A

Most people, farmers especially, have to work very hard to earn money.

King Solomon teaches us: "Do not be lazy. Work hard. Save your money."

Show Illustration 8B

It is important to save money. Some people save money by putting it in the bank. Others hide their money. Solomon did not say it is wrong to have money. He does teach that it is wrong to get money dishonestly. (See 11:1; 20:10, 23; 28:6.)

It is easy for rich people to become proud. They feel as if they do not need God. So King Solomon warns, "Those who trust in their riches will fall" (11:28). "Do not wear yourself out trying to get rich. Do not set your eyes on money. Money will sprout wings and flyaway like an eagle," Solomon taught. (See 23:4-5.

Show Illustration 8C

King Solomon warned, "Riches and money will not last forever. It is easy for the rich to forget God and ask, 'The LORD? Who is He?'" (See 30:8-9.)

It was the Lord who blessed Solomon with great riches. He also blesses some today with much money. And He can teach us how to use what He provides. Since everything (whether little or much) comes from God, we are to honor Him with our money. We honor Him by giving to our church.

Show Illustration 8D

Our money should also be used to help missions and missionaries.

We should share our money with poor people. And we should most certainly pay our bills! (See 3:9, 11:24-26; Matthew 6:19-20.)

God has taught us much through King Solomon. Now it is time for you to look into your heart. Is the sin of pride there? If so, will you confess that pride to the Lord right now? He wants you to humble yourself. *(Teacher:* Read any of these verses: Matthew 23:12; James 4:6, 10; 1 Peter 5:5-6.)

Do you love money more than you love God? Do you keep your money for yourself? Do you give to God as you should? Ask the Lord to help you make the right choices this week. Humble yourself so you can have an attitude which honors Him.

(Teacher: Allow a quiet time for prayer as students examine their hearts.)

Lesson 3
WISDOM FOR THE FAMILY

NOTE TO THE TEACHER

In addition to his proverbs, Solomon wrote 1005 songs (1 Kings 4:32). One of his songs is the Bible book entitled *The Song of Solomon*. This song teaches the holiness and beauty of marriage. It emphasizes this: God planned for one man and one woman to be married for life. (Compare: Genesis 2:22-24; Matthew 19:5-6; 1 Corinthians 7:39; Ephesians 5:31.) In *The Song of Solomon* and in *Proverbs*, God tells how to have a godly marriage and family.

Many marriages and families are not God-like. So your students must learn God's standards and commands for the family. His specific instructions are recorded in these two books of Solomon's. We need to emphasize and heed these teachings. They are an important part of God's holy Word.

On illustration 11, print the following words on lines indicated.

Center of top dotted line: Discipline
11a	Discipline Hated
11-1	Foolish Child
11-2	Mother Ashamed
11-3	Father Ruined
11b	Discipline Learned
11-4	Wise Child
11-5	Happy Child
11-6	Happy Family

(Teacher: By prIntmg these words yourself, you will better remember them. Also, you will be helping teachers in other lands who use these illustrations. Because they cannot speak English, we leave the spaces blank for their languages. Some of these volumes are presently used in more than 40 tongues. Would you breathe a prayer for this global outreach?)

On a chalkboard, print: *Rules for a Happy Marriage*. (See lesson point #2.)

Throughout this lesson, the words he, him, his, arc used. The teaching is equally feminine.

Family worship is emphasized in the close of this lesson. If you need additional help, write to the publishers of this volume.

Scripture to be studied: The Song of Solomon; verses in Proverbs.

The *aim* of the lesson: To emphasize God's perfect plan for the family.

What your students should *know*: God who created the family gave commands for family living.

What your students should *feel*: A desire to follow God's guidelines for family life.

What your students should *do*: Determine to make their family life happy.

Lesson outline (for the teacher's and students' notebooks):
1. Love in the family (The Song of Solomon; verses from Proverbs).
2. Children in the family (See verses mentioned in lesson).
3. Discipline in the family (See verses in lesson).
4. Joy in the family (See verses in lesson).

The verse to be memorized:

The fear of the LORD is the beginning of wisdom and knowledge of the Holy is understanding. (Proverbs 9:10)

THE LESSON

Today we learn about the family. What is a family? (Encourage student response to all questions.) Do you belong to a family? Who is in your family? Who created the first family? *(God)* Who was in that family? (Read Genesis 2:22-24.) How many wives did God give to Adam? *(Only one, Eve)* And God commanded Adam to be true and loyal to Eve.

Adam and Eve had children. Do you remember their names? *(Cain, Abel, Seth)* They had other children, too. (See Genesis 4:1-5, 25; 5:4.)

Why do you think God created the family? (Encourage response.) Here is one reason for God's creating the family: The children would grow up and have other children. (See Genesis 1:26-28.) God planned it this way so many people could enjoy His wonderful world.

Here is another reason God created the family: Those in the family would love and give happiness to other family members. God wants your family to be happy and to live honorably. And He tells how you can have this kind of family life.

When we play games, we must follow the rules. To have a happy family life, we must know and obey God's rules. And God used wise King Solomon to guide families. Before you hear the rules, listen to this:

1. LOVE IN THE FAMILY

From the book of *Proverbs,* we learn some of the wisdom God gave Solomon. He also wrote more than 1,000 songs. One of his songs is the Bible book called *The Song of Solomon*. It is King Solomon's own love story about which he sang.

Great, wealthy, wise King Solomon could marry anyone he chose. One day he saw a young shepherdess working in a field. And he sang, "She is beautiful!" He thought, *I have to meet her.* And he did.

Show Illustration #9

King Solomon and the shepherdess visited together often. They soon became good friends. In time, they loved each other very much. King Solomon sang to the shepherdess: "You are the fairest [the most attractive] woman." (See Song of Solomon 1:8, 15.)

The shepherdess whispered, "O King, you are fair [attractive]." (See Song of Solomon 1:16.)

The king and shepherdess always spoke nicely to each other. They never said harsh, unkind, critical words.

When they were apart, they wished to be together. (See Song of Solomon 2:8-9.)

To herself, the shepherdess thought, *I belong to my dear one and he belongs to me. We belong to each other.* (See Song of Solomon 2:16; 6:3; 7:10.) These two were true to one another. They belonged only to each other, no one else.

Love is one of the most wonderful gifts God gives us. We all want to be loved. Children want to be loved by their parents. Parents want the love of their children. And husbands and wives want each other's love.

King Solomon truly loved the young shepherdess. Because of their love for each other, arrangements were made for their wedding. They waited awhile. But during that waiting time, they neither lived together nor went to bed together. That would have been sin. God says that only *after* two people are married, should they go to bed together. (See 1 Corinthians 6:18; Galatians 5:19; Hebrews 13:4.) The Lord sees and knows everything. And He severely punishes those who disobey Him. (See Proverbs 5:1-6, 20-23; 15:3, 9-10.)

Finally the handsome, wise king and the lovely shepherdess were married. Now they belonged to each other–they were one. (See Matthew 19:5-6.) How happy they were! The king's wife exclaimed, "My husband is more handsome than 10,000 others!" (See Song of Solomon 5:10.)

King Solomon sang to his bride, "You are beautiful. And oh, how pleasing!" (See Song of Solomon 7:6.) The longer they were married, the more their love grew.

Do you know why King Solomon and his wife were so happy? Because they had not broken three of *God's Rules for a Happy Marriage:*

Rule #1: NEVER go to bed with anyone but the one to whom you are married. (See Leviticus 18:20; 20:10; Proverbs 5:7-23; Hebrews 13:4.)

Rule #2: ALWAYS love the person you married. (See Proverbs 5:18.)

Rule #3: NEVER even LOOK at someone else wishing you could make love to that person. (See Deuteronomy 5:21; Matthew 5:27-28.)

(Teacher: Have students repeat these three rules and write them in their notebooks.)

You may not be married now. But perhaps some day you will marry. So be sure to remember these rules. Talk about them at home today. If these guidelines are broken, everyone is hurt. Everyone is unhappy. And God does not bless anyone who disobeys His commands.

Wise King Solomon said: "He who finds a wife, finds what is good. And he receives favor from the Lord" (Proverbs 18:22). "A wise wife is from the Lord" (Proverbs 19:14). When he was old, Solomon added, "Live happily with your wife" (Ecclesiastes 9:9).

God's Word says that a good wife "works hard and takes care of their family. She saves money. She helps the poor." And, most important, "she fears the Lord." (See Proverbs 31:10-30.) This kind of wife, God says, will be praised by her husband. (See Proverbs 31:28.)

A husband and wife who honestly obey God will be truly happy.

2. CHILDREN IN THE FAMILY

Did you know that you were a gift from God to your parents? King Solomon wrote, "Children are a gift–a reward–from the Lord." (See Psalm 127:3.) Do you think you have always been a good gift? Are you an honorable reward? (Let students discuss how sons and daughters–at any age–can make their parents happy.)

Show Illustration #10

King Solomon wrote many proverbs for children. (All references which follow are from Proverbs unless otherwise noted.) Solomon commanded, "Listen to your father and mother." (See 1:8-9; 2:1-5.) "Do not forget what they teach you." (See 3:1.) "Remember their words." (See 4:1-10.) "Obey your father and mother." (See 6:20-24.)

Should children obey only when they feel like it? *(No!)* "A wise son [or daughter] always listens to what the father teaches." (See 13:1.)

Sternly, King Solomon taught: "A foolish son [who acts as if there is no God] is a heartache to his mother." (See 10:1; 15:20; 17:21, 25; 19:26.) But how different it is when children obey their parents. King Solomon exclaimed, "They make their father and mother happy!" (See 23:24-25; 29:3a.) Obedient children are also happy, for God blesses obedience. (See 1:8-9; 2:1-12; 3:1-6; 4:8-10.)

3. DISCIPLINE IN THE FAMILY

God gave commands to children. He also gives this important command to fathers: "Train up a child in the way he should go. And when he is old, he will not depart from it" (22:6). Fathers and mothers are responsible to God for their children. They must teach their children the right way to live. They have to teach their children to become "wise." What kind of a person is wise? *(Teacher:* Review from lesson #1, using illustration 3a.)

Through Solomon, God teaches fathers and mothers: "Discipline [punish or correct] your child. If you do not, it proves you do not love your child. Parents who truly love their children discipline them." (See 13:24.) "Your children will not die if you punish them. If you punish them now, God may not need to punish them forever." (See 23:13-14.) "Scolding and sometimes even spanking children, help them to learn." (See 29:15.) "Discipline your children and they will make you very happy." (See 29:17.)

So parents are responsible to punish their disobedient children. Parents who do not do so, disobey God.

Show Illustration #11

Through Solomon, God says this about a child who hates discipline:

1. "That child is foolish." (Point to #11-1.) Anyone who hates discipline, crosses God out of his life. Such a person is senseless. (See 15:5a; compare 15:10.)

2. "That child makes his mother ashamed." (Show 11-2.) A child who hates discipline, disgraces and shames his mother. (See 29:15b.)

3. "That child ruins his father." (Show 11-3.) A child who hates discipline crushes his father. (See 19:13a.)

King Solomon has this good news for those who learn from discipline:

1. "They are wise." (Show #11-4.) A child who accepts discipline has good sense. (See 13:1a; 15:5, 31-32; 19:20.)
2. "They are happy because God blesses them." (Show 11-5.) The child who accepts discipline receives favor from God. (See 8:32.)
3. "They make their parenrs happy." (Show 11-6.) The child who accepts discipline brings *joy* to his parents. (See 23:24-25; 29:17.)

4. JOY IN THE FAMILY

Suppose the Lord Jesus came to visit your home. Would you be glad to invite Him in? Is there anything you would change? Would you listen to the same radio or television programs? Would you want to hide some of your books? Would you want Him to see what you are eating or drinking? Would *you* talk to Him just as you speak to your family? Would you be happy to have Christ Jesus with you? Or would you be ashamed?

Did you know that the Lord sees everything in your home? And He knows all that is going on. "The eyes of the LORD are in every place, seeing the evil and the good." (See 5:21; 15:3.)

Would you and your family like to please God? If so, each one must belong to Him. You can belong to Him by receiving the Lord Jesus as Saviour. When you receive Him, He forgives your sins. And God receives you into His family.

When you belong to God's family, you will want to read His Book, the Bible. God wants fathers to lead their families in studying His Word together. (See Deuteronomy 6:6-9.) Ask your parents if once each day your family can have family worship. Together *you* can read God's Word and sing and pray. The Lord is pleased when He hears you pray. (See 15:8b.) Ask Him to help you to tell others about Jesus Christ. (See 11:30.) God loves those who diligently, earnestly seek Him. (See 8:17.) He has blessed many, many families who worship Him together.

Show Illustration #12

Do you truly trust in the Lord and obey Him? If so, He will be a fortress–a strong tower–to protect you. (Read 18:10.) You can run to Him whenever you need His help.

The Lord will also be a shield to guard you. (See 2:7-9.) When Satan tempts you, God Himself is willing to shield you. (Read Ephesians 6:11-17.) And Satan's fiery darts will not harm you. (Read Proverbs 3:26.) "Happy is the person who trusts in the LORD." (See 16:20.)

Are you and your family trusting in the Lord? If some do not know Him, will you pray for them right now? Then ask the Lord how you can bring happiness to your family.

Lesson 4
WISDOM OF THIS WORLD

NOTE TO THE TEACHER

In Bible order, Solomon's books are *Proverbs, Ecclesiastes, The Song of Solomon*. Solomon's Song is the story of his youthful love. Ecclesiastes records his thoughts in old age. For this reason, in this study these two books are reversed from biblical order.

When Solomon was young, he obeyed God. He became the world's wisest, richest, man. Later he turned from the Lord and disobeyed His commands. (See 1 Kings 11:1-43.) He took many, many wives (See Song of Solomon 6:8.) And he turned from worshiping the living God to lifeless idols. We have studied some of the excellent rules which God caused Solomon to write. But Solomon himself did not obey these rules. So God severely punished him by later tearing apart his kingdom.

Solomon never found life meaningful after he turned from the LORD Jehovah. Ecclesiastes shows how empty life is without a relationship to the LORD. The aged Solomon tried to find answers to life's problems. He looked "under the sun . . . under Heaven . . . and on the earth." But true answers come from above–from the LORD Himself.

"All Scripture is given by inspiration of God, and is profitable . . ." (See 2 Timothy 3:16.) Therefore it is important to study Ecclesiastes. It is a warning to all that turning from the LORD ends in emptiness. Solomon knew this: "Fear God and obey Him. One day God will judge everything you do. He will even judge hidden things, both good and evil." (See Ecclesiastes 12:13-14.) It is imperative that your students understand these truths.

Before teaching this lesson, review previous studies. Emphasize whatever is appropriate for your group.

On a large poster, print *God's Laws for Kings*. (See beginning of this lesson.)

Scripture to be studied: Deuteronomy 17: 14-20; 1 Kings 10:14-11:43; Ecclesiastes 1:1-12:14

The *aim* of the lesson: To show that life without God means nothing.

What your students should *know*: That God alone gives joy and satisfaction.

What your students should *feel*: A desire for divine wisdom, rather than the wisdom of this world.

What your students should *do*: Daily remember and honor God, their Creator.

Lesson outline (for the teacher's and students' notebooks):

1. Solomon's foolishness (1 Kings 10:26-11:43).
2. Solomon's foolish search (Ecclesiastes 1:1-2:26).
3. Solomon's old-age thoughts (See verses from Ecclesiastes).
4. Solomon's advice (See verses in lesson).

The verse to be memorized:

The fear of the LORD is the beginning of wisdom and knowledge of the Holy is understanding. (Proverbs 9:10)

THE LESSON:

We have been studying Solomon's life. Have you liked him? Why? *(He loved the LORD and obeyed Him. He used his wisdom to rule his people well. He worshiped the LORD with many sacrifices. He was a good leader of God's people.)*

I wish I could tell you that Solomon always obeyed God until he died. But did he? Listen carefully.

Long before Solomon lived, God gave laws for the kings of the Jews. These were written in God's Law. So people and kings knew His laws. (See Deuteronomy 17:14-20.) *(Teacher: Display poster.)*

God's Laws for Kings
Deuteronomy 17:14-20

1. Israel's king must be a Jew whom God has chosen (verse 15).
2. The king must not have many horses. He must not get horses from Egypt (verse 16).
3. The king must not have many wives (verse 17).
4. The king must not have stacks of gold and silver (verse 17).
5. The king must make a copy of all of God's Law for himself. And he must read God's Law (verses 18-20).

King Solomon knew and understood all these laws. When he first became king of Israel, he obeyed them. And the LORD blessed him and his people.

1. SOLOMON'S FOOLISHNESS
1 Kings 10:26-11:43

King Solomon could never break Law #1, for he was a Jew. And God had chosen him to be king. (See 1 Chronicles 28:5.)

In time, Solomon seemingly forgot the last part of Law #5. He was disobeying God's Law. So he could not have been reading it every day. For example, he wanted horses to make his army strong. (See 1 Kings 10:26, 28.) And guess where he got his horses. *From Egypt!* So he broke Law #2. Instead of trusting God for protection, he gathered a strong army. Now he had what the other kings of his world had.

God had always meant for a man to have only one wife. And the man and wife would be one. God said. (See Genesis 2:21-24; compare Ephesians 5:31-32.) This was in God's Law which Solomon knew.

Show Illustration #13

But Solomon had one wife, then another and another–even hundreds of wives! (See 1 Kings 11:1-3.) So King Solomon broke Law #3.

Solomon's foreign wives did not love the true and living God. They worshiped idols [false gods]. One wife might have whispered, "Solomon, I want to burn incense to my idol. Please build an altar for it." So Solomon, God's king, had the altar built.

When the other wives saw this altar, what do you suppose happened? *They all wanted altars for their idols.* So Solomon had many altars built. He even worshiped his wives' idols!

God had commanded all His people, "You shall have no other gods but Me." (See Exodus 20:3-5.) King Solomon should have been a good example to his people. Instead, he turned from the living God to idols made by men. (See 1 Kings 11:3-8.) Solomon proudly, deliberately, chose to go his own way. He turned away from God.

When Solomon first became king, God had promised to make him very wise. He also promised the king great riches. (See 2 Chronicles 1:11-12.) God kept His promise, you may be certain. But Solomon was not satisfied. He kept collecting gold and silver and stacking it up for himself. (See 1 Kings 9:27-28; 10:10-11,14-22,27; Ecclesaistes 2:8.) So Solomon broke Law #4.

Do you remember the promise God had given Solomon years before? He said, "Solomon, obey My laws. *If* you do, your family will always sit on the throne of Israel." God had also given this warning: "Solomon, if you turn away from Me and worship other gods, I shall take the kingdom from you." (See 1 Kings 9:4-7.)

God always *means* what He says. And God always *does* what He says. After King Solomon died, his great kingdom was torn apart. His son ruled over only a very little part of the kingdom. (See 1 Kings 11:31-32.) And later, that little part was seized by an enemy nation. (See Jeremiah 39:8-10.)

2. SOLOMON'S FOOLISH SEARCH
Ecclesiastes 1:1-2:26

When Solomon grew old, he thought about all he had done in his life. Was he sorry he had disobeyed God and turned from Him? We are not told. But God caused him to write another Bible book, Ecclesiastes. In it Solomon warns us not to make the same mistakes he made.

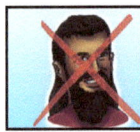

Show Illustration #14A

Old King Solomon now understood that life without God is empty. It has no meaning, no purpose. Without God, there is no real happiness.

Listen to what King Solomon said, "I thought if I knew everything in the world, I would be happy." Remember! God made Solomon the wisest man in his world. So he studied and learned more and more.

Show Illustration #14B

But King Solomon moaned, "Wisdom is not making me happy. All my hard study was like chasing the wind, trying to catch it." (See Ecclesiastes 1:12-14, 16-17. *Teacher:* All references which follow are from Ecclesiastes, unless otherwise stated.) It is good to study and learn as much as possible. But without God in your life, learning can be like wind-chasing. God is the One who makes all learning really worthwhile.

Let me ask you some questions. *(Teacher: Encourage student response.)*

If you had lots and lots of money, would you be happy?

If you lived in a big, beautiful house, would you be happy?

If you could go to many places and have fun, would you be happy?

King Solomon thought that if he had everything he wanted, he would be very happy.

Show Illustration #14C

So the king decided, "I shall build houses and plant vineyards for myself. I shall have beautiful gardens and fruit trees. I shall make watering ponds. I shall have many servants to care for everything. I shall gather flocks, herds of animals, silver and gold. I shall have musicians–singers and those who play instruments." King Solomon had everything he wanted.

(See 2:4-10,) Now, was he the happiest man in the world?

Listen to what the king said, "As I looked at everything, it was useless. It was like chasing the wind. There was nothing worthwhile anywhere." (See 2:11.) Solomon had turned from God and left Him out of his life.

King Solomon was never lazy. He worked hard. He had been in charge of building God's magnificent temple. And it took 13 years to build his palace. (See 1 Kings 7:1.) Solomon also wrote thousands of proverbs and hundreds of songs. (See 1 Kings 4:32.) He ruled over a large kingdom. Yet when he was old he was not happy. Why? Because he turned from God and left Him out of his life. He was no longer wise.

King Solomon knew he would die some day. Then everything he owned would be left to others. To himself, he thought, *They will not appreciate all I have done. They might not take care of anything. And I can do nothing about it. All my hard work will be empty and meaningless.* (See 2:18-21.)

So King Solomon cried, "Nothing brings happiness." (See 1:16-18.) The king had turned from God. So everything was worthless.

3. SOLOMON'S OLD-AGE THOUGHTS

Shortly before he died, King Solomon wrote down his thoughts. Here are some of them.

Show Illustration #15A
Solomon thought:

#1. *'I could never get enough of anything to satisfy me. I always wanted more–more silver, more gold, more book-learning.* (See 5:10-11.)

Show Illustration #15B
#2. *Everyone on earth sins.* (See 7:20; compare Romans 3:23, 6:23.)

Show Illustration #15C
#3. *No one can stop death. Everyone will die some day.* (See 8:8; 2:16; 12:5, 7.)

Show Ilustration #1D
#4. *When we die, we leave everything here.* (See 2:18, 21; 5:15-16.)

Show Illustration #15E
#5. *We shall all be judged by God.* (See 3:16-17; 11:9; 12:14.)

Why did King Solomon have such thoughts when he was about to die? He had turned away from God and disobeyed His laws. (See, for example, Song of Solomon 6:8.) He had deliberately left the LORD out of his life. So the thoughts of dying and standing before God, the Judge, troubled him.

4. SOLOMON'S ADVICE

Show Illustration #16

Old Solomon left these final reminders: "Remember your Creator while you are young, before days of trouble come to you. Fear [reverence, trust] God and obey His commandments. For He will judge everything, even hidden things, both good and evil." (See 12:1, 13-14.)

God had made young Solomon very, very wise. But Solomon turned away from God. He married many wives. He did not always serve God. He sometimes worshiped idols. In these sinful actions, he clearly disobeyed God's law. Foolish, foolish Solomon!

Do you belong to God by having trusted Christ as your Saviour? If so, God has given you wisdom. (See 1 Corinthians 1:26-30.) Are you using your wisdom? Are you wise enough to obey God and His laws? Are you using wisely the money God has entrusted to you? If God allows honor to come to you, do you accept that honor wisely?

Show Illustration #3

In which group do you belong–the WISE or the FOOLISH? The wise receive their wisdom from the Lord. Foolish people follow the sinful wisdom of this world.

Everyone in all the world has sinned. And sin separates us from God. But Jesus took our punishment for sin by dying on the cross. Because He is God's Son, He arose from the dead. Anyone who truly believes in Him can have forgiveness of sin. Do you want God to forgive your sin? If so, you can have His forgiveness this very day. Will you talk with me about this after class? *(Teacher:* Be available to spend time with those who remain.)

Are you already a child of God? If so, are you wisely honoring the Lord and obeying His Word? If not, will you right now talk silently to Him, your Creator? *(Teacher:* Allow a time of quiet for students to talk with the Lord.)

www.ingramcontent.com/pod-product-compliance
Lightning Source LLC
Chambersburg PA
CBHW060806090426
42736CB00002B/179